the threads of becoming

the threads of becoming

a memoir in poems

tamara hill

Copyright © 2025 by Tamara Hill

All rights reserved.

No part of this book may be reproduced, or stored in a retrieval system, or transmitted in any form or by any means, electronic, mechanical, photocopying, recording, or otherwise, without express written permission of the publisher.

Without in any way limiting the author's and publisher's exclusive rights under copyright, any use of this publication to "train" generative artificial intelligence (AI) technologies to generate text is expressly prohibited. The author reserves all rights to license uses of this work for generative AI training and development of machine learning language models.

Some names and identifying details have been changed to protect the privacy of individuals.

Published by GFB™, Seattle
www.girlfridayproductions.com

Produced by Girl Friday Productions

Cover design: Emily Weigel
Interior design: Rachel Marek

Image credits: cover, © The Escape of Malee/Shutterstock

ISBN (hardcover): 978-1-967510-72-6
ISBN (ebook): 978-1-967510-73-3

Library of Congress Control Number: 2025912156

First edition

*For Mona, who taught me resilience with grace,
and whose quiet strength still carries me.*

For Conor and Allie, the rhythm of my heart, my courage in motion, my reminder that love—true love—never waivers.

This is for you.

contents

Introduction xi

part 1: beginning and belonging

The Magic of Beginnings 3
The Empty Door 5
The Silence Between Smiles 6
Whispering Goodbye 8
A Love That Simply Knows 10
Cutting Class with Ted 12
A Subtle Champion 14
What Would Mona Do? 16
South of Somewhere 18
Finding Home 20

part 2: motherhood and transformation

The Simplicity of You 25
Bound by Love 27
My Miracle 29
A Little Spitfire 31
The Space Between Us 33
Hope, the Tenth 35
A Good Decision 37
A Playful Tug-a-Tumble 39
The Asking 41

part 3: finding purpose in creativity, travel, and career

The Flow of a Dream 47
Code and Soul 49
The Trails We Keep 51
Elegant and the Echo 53
The Parisi Table 56
Wheels of Discovery 58
The Cliff's Edge 60
The Journey Within 62
A Journey of Creation 64
The Day Fate Wrapped Us Together 66
Standing Ovation 68
The Shape of a Dream 70

part 4: love and letting go

A Bond Divided 75
The Quiet Cage 77
The Mask 79
First Love, Forever Fond 81
Still Waiting 83
The Love of Family 85
Rest Easy, Diane 87
A Dream, Misunderstood 90

part 5: resilience and reflection

Ladder 25 95
Awake in the Dark 98
A View from the Hills 100

The Echo in Her Mind	102
The Last Ride	104
Through the Stuckness	106
The Voices in My Ear	107
Grief's Drive	109
Seeking the Lighter Path	111
I Want	113
A Meeting That Changed the Map	115
Full Circle	117
What I Choose Now	119
The Turning	121
The Thread of Maybe	124
About the Author	127

introduction

I have always been woven from stories—threads of longing and belonging, of love, loss, resilience, and hope. *The Threads of Becoming* is my attempt to gather these fragments, to trace the quiet transformations, the moments of triumph and surrender, that have shaped the woman I am today.

This book began not as poetry, but as a traditional memoir. Yet as life kept unfolding, with new layers of reflection, grief, joy, and becoming, it was clear that a linear story could not capture it. Poetry, with its ability to hold a lifetime in a moment, became the truest form. These poems do not move chronologically—they move by heart, by memory, by the invisible pull of what matters most.

I grew up in the Bay Area of California, a child of divorce, toggling between the independence of my mother's home and weekends spent with my father, who remained a steady confidant until his passing from Parkinson's disease five years ago. Much of my early life was spent dreaming—manifesting a future where creativity, connection, and beauty would be at the center. In those long, quiet hours, I learned the power of imagination and the quiet courage of hope.

My grandparents, especially my grandmother Mona, offered me my first true sanctuary. In their kitchen, over buttered toast and perfectly cooled hot chocolate, I learned what it meant to be seen and cherished without condition. When Mona fell ill, I chose to stay close, attending college nearby,

introduction

holding her hand through her final breath. That moment changed everything about how I would love, how I would lose, and how I would live—a moment that would echo in everything I built thereafter.

The poems in these pages travel through time, from the bittersweet friendships of youth, to the early days of a pioneering digital career. I found success at a young age but carried deep, private grief alongside it. Life taught me early that ambition and heartbreak are often stitched together.

Motherhood opened me wider than anything else could. My son, born in New York City, and my daughter, born in Berkeley two years later, became my living reminders of purpose and grace. Watching them grow—so close in age, yet even closer in bond—has been one of my greatest privileges. Together, they form the truest legacy of love I could ever hope to leave behind—certainly one of my proudest achievements.

There were seasons of love and seasons of letting go.

Tamara with her children, Conor and Allie, along with their dog, Hope, outside her first Italian property in Puglia.

introduction

My divorce, though painful, became a doorway into deeper freedom—an invitation to rebuild myself, to trust my own voice again, to create a life centered on joy and purpose rather than survival alone.

After my years in corporate America, leading innovation in tech, hospitality, and design, the COVID-19 pandemic brought an unexpected turning point. A layoff gave me space to imagine a new life—one built on creativity, connection, and community. I founded the Hill House Group, designing and developing luxury hospitality properties and experiences, first in California and now in Puglia, Italy, where I live part of the year. Through this work, I have found a way to merge my love of real estate, art, storytelling, and a deeper sense of place.

Our properties have thrived, helping to redefine travel for both solo explorers and families seeking beauty, connection, and meaning. My next project, a B&B in Puglia, is already taking root—a dream stitched from all the experiences, risks, and reinventions that brought me so far.

Friendship, too, has been a sustaining thread. Across decades and continents, I have been blessed by the unwavering light of true friends—those who remind me that connection transcends geography, that shared laughter and trust can bridge even the longest distances. Their presence has been a quiet symphony in the background of my becoming.

And still, there are dreams I hold tenderly. I remain open to finding that one true love—a partner who sees both the strength and the softness in me. Yet I stand whole in my own company, knowing that fulfillment is not dependent on being chosen, but on choosing myself again and again.

The Threads of Becoming is not simply a collection of poems. It is a map of healing, of wonder, of surviving and thriving. It is a reflection of the messy, beautiful, imperfect life we all are stitching, every day, from the threads we are given.

I hope these poems meet you where you are. I hope they

introduction

invite you to see the richness in your own story—the losses survived, the loves held, the dreams dared, the resilience you may not even realize you've built.

Let these words move through you. Let them tug at the loose threads of your heart and weave something new.

Welcome to *The Threads of Becoming*.

Tamara

part 1

beginning and belonging

the magic of beginnings

From the start, they were who they are,
Each a distinct and radiant star.
One danced softly in the womb's embrace,
The other, a fire with a lively pace.

Their births mirrored their souls so true,
One calm, one bold, each spirit knew.
Quiet days alone, just them and me,
Revealed their worlds as they came to be.

The way they gazed, the way they cried,
Their laughter unique, their fears beside.
I watched their bond, a gentle thread,
The way they loved, the words unsaid.

Each year, I write, with pen in hand,
A letter that marks where they stand.
Their joys, their growth, the paths they've tried,
The triumphs, the tears, the times they've cried.

I see in those words, with each new page,
How nature blooms and grows with age.
They've always been innately true,
Yet life has shaped and colored their hue.

The nurture guides, the lessons teach,
Through beauty and challenge, they both reach.
They bend, they shift, but at their core,
They remain the souls I knew before.

It's a wonder, a gift, this human way,
To see how life sculpts the clay.
As a mother, I stand in awe,
Witnessing life's most perfect law.

For beginnings are shared by us all,
A nature innate, yet shaped by the call
Of nurture's hand, both gentle and strong,
The balance that carries us all along.

And so, I cherish this truth I've found,
That in their hearts, they're always sound.
Their nature, their nurture, intertwined,
A magical reality, endlessly divine.

the empty door

As a young girl, I came home to an empty place,
no open arms, no warm embrace.
Just quiet halls and shadows deep,
a house where silence learned to creep.

The doors would close, the locks would turn,
a child left alone to yearn.
Her face was there but out of reach,
a love I sought she couldn't teach.

So in my mind, I built a sky,
a brighter world where dreams could fly.
A place where hearts were never cold,
and all the warmth I craved took hold.

The empty door taught me to see
the strength I'd need to set me free.
And from that silence, I took flight,
to find my own and make it right.

the silence between smiles

You could see it in the way I'd stand,
a shrinking child, a trembling hand.
The laughter gone, replaced by fears,
a quiet mask to hide the tears.

The photos held what words could not,
a fading spark, a vacant spot.
My shoulders hunched, my gaze turned low,
a child too young to feel the blow.

But Grandmother came, my saving grace,
with gentle words, a warm embrace.
Her car became a safe retreat,
her home, the place my heart could beat.

She saw the truth, she knew the cost,
the weight I bore, the love I'd lost.
Her steady voice became my guide,
her arms, the place my dreams could hide.

From whispers grew a stronger me,
her faith unbound, her love the key.
The silence broke, the smiles returned,
and through her care, a life was earned.

whispering goodbye

I was raised by a love steady and true,
My grandmother's arms, the whole world I knew.
Through childhood storms and teenage fears,
Her wisdom was there, through laughter and tears.

Each Wednesday, we'd share our own special rite,
Painting nails, talking dreams deep into the night.
Stories and wishes, exchanged with care,
A bond so profound, few could compare.

But illness came, slow and unkind,
A shadow that lingered, heavy in mind.
For three long years, I stayed by her side,
A caretaker, companion, love magnified.

When college loomed, with my dreams in view,
My heart ached for the parting I knew.
And as hospice spoke of her final hour,
They said she was clinging with stubborn power.

"It's time," they whispered. "Someone must say,
It's okay for her to slip away."
I was chosen, my heart a storm,
To give her strength in a final form.

I entered the room, held her hand tight,
Swallowed my pain, found the words that felt right.
In her ear, I whispered, "You can let go,
Everything you taught me, I already know.

"I'll carry your wisdom, your strength, your grace;
I'll live for us both, in every space.
You've given me all that I need to stand;
Now it's my turn to hold your hand."

Inside, I ached, the tears fought to rise,
But I kept my promise, no wavering cries.
A strength like that came from a deep, sacred place,
As my grandmother's soul found its final embrace.

Her last breath came, soft as a sigh,
A release, a farewell, under the sky.
And in that moment, as pain ran wild,
Grandmother's strength was passed to grandchild.

a love that simply knows

The day she was born, he quietly said,
"You are enough"—words she tucked in her head.
To him, love was simple, without demand,
A quiet certainty, a steady hand.

In that simplicity, she found her place,
A shelter, a warmth, an endless grace.
No need to impress, no battles to win,
His pride started where her life did begin.

Yet sometimes she wished he'd look and see
The deeper layers of who she could be—
The restless heart, the dreams untold,
The silent prayers she dared to hold.

But with time, she saw the gift he gave:
A love that let her be wild and brave.
No need to shape, no need to confine,
Only to stand by, steady and kind.

Now she hopes to find someone who knows
The beauty in strength, the grace in her lows.
Someone who holds her when tears freely fall,
Who lifts her spirit through it all—
Who knows that tenderness is not a flaw,
But the bravest language the heart can draw.

And as her life continues to unfold,
She longs for a love both fierce and bold—
A man who sees her, all she can be,
And loves her with unguarded clarity.

For from her father, she learned what's true:
Love doesn't bind; it lets you bloom.
It doesn't seek to fix or impose.
It simply trusts. It simply knows.

cutting class with ted

Of all the memories high school left behind,
It's the small ones that linger, vivid in mind.
Friendships, classes, dreams untold,
Antics and drama that never grow old.

Closest to my heart, honest and free,
Are the days we cut class, just Ted and me.
My beat-up Plymouth Duster, a clunky old charm,
Became our escape, our freedom alarm.

We'd head for donuts, no care for the time,
The sweetest rebellion, a rhythm, a rhyme.
Over parking lot speed bumps, we'd fly with a laugh,
Fast turns and detours, a carefree path.

It wasn't romance, just something more rare,
A bond of laughter, a friendship to share.
Sports in common, the jokes we'd repeat,
The way I felt safe, just me in my seat.

For in those moments, no roles to fulfill,
I was the tomboy, just me, at will.
No need to impress, no games to play,
Ted let me be me, in the simplest way.

We'd smuggle the donuts back to the room,
Late to class, but never with gloom.
Our giggles would echo, our joy would show,
A fleeting rebellion, a bond we'd grow.

Now, years have passed, the memories fade,
But Ted and those donuts, the friendship we made,
Still live in my heart, a treasure so true,
A high school memory I always renew.

For it's not the big moments that define the past,
But the ones where we laughed, where freedom would last.
And class cutting with Ted, treats in our hand,
Is a piece of my soul, forever unplanned.

a subtle champion

She stood on the court, racket in hand,
The bounce of the ball, the feel of the sand.
The cheers of others filled the air,
But familiar faces never were there.

Match after match, she'd play alone,
Her victories quiet, her triumphs unknown.
Yet her grandmother would always ask,
"How did you do?" her tone a mask.

The girl would smile and shrug it away,
"It's okay, Grandma; it's just another day."
But the elder knew, with wisdom deep,
The longing her granddaughter tried to keep.

So one day, with purpose, she made her way,
To the edge of the court where the girl would play.
No grand announcement, no loud applause,
Just a subtle figure, defying the laws.

The girl saw her there, just a peek by the fence,
Her grandmother's love, quiet yet immense.
A head tilted slightly, a hand on the wire,
A presence so simple, yet lifting her higher.

In that moment, she felt it all,
The strength to rise, the courage to fall.
Her heart beat steady, her game took flight,
And she played the best match of her life that night.

Every serve, every swing, had a purpose anew,
Her grandmother's gaze pulling her through.
She was seen, understood, cherished and known,
A love that stood firm without being shown.

And when the match ended, her victory clear,
She felt not just pride, but a love so near.
Her grandmother's smile was soft, not grand,
But it held the world in the palm of her hand.

For champions aren't made by courts or acclaim,
But by those who stand quietly, calling your name.
And in that match, on that ordinary day,
Her grandmother's love lit up the way.

what would mona do?

When I was young and the day felt long,
I'd dream of a place where I belonged.
School could wait; my heart would soar—
Imagining Grandma at the door.

In her car, she'd sit with a gentle smile,
Ready to rescue me, mile by mile.
Friends would ask, "Will you come to play?"
But I'd shake my head, light on display.

"No, I'm going to Grandma's," I'd gleefully say,
For her love made every shadow fade away.
She was my compass, my truest guide,
My rock, in whom I would confide.

When twenty came, the world turned gray,
For Mona, my anchor, had drifted away.
But her spirit stayed, a whisper near,
In moments of doubt, her voice I'd hear.

"What would Mona do?" I'd quietly ask,
When life felt like an impossible task.
Her wisdom, her strength, her loving grace,
Still guide me now, though I can't see her face.

Oh, how I wish she could see me today,
Meet my children, watch them play.
I hope she knows, in her endless light,
I've lived for her, with all my might.

Every step, every dream pursued,
I hope would make her pride renewed.
For in my heart, her love shines through,
And every voice whispers, "What would Mona do?"

Mona, my guardian, my North Star,
Though you've gone, you're never far.
I carry your love in all I do,
Hoping each day to honor you.

south of somewhere

At sixteen I flew with stars in my eyes,
To a place where the lavender kissed the skies.
South of France, with ten from my school,
We chased a year like a sparkling jewel.

Jenny beside me, my anchor, my flame.
Best friends before—now more than a name.
We landed with backpacks, hope in our hands,
Ready to run through these foreign lands.

Kids from all over, voices a blend,
Strangers at first, soon more than just friends.
French in the morning, café au lait,
Laughing in lessons, dreaming all day.

My French maman said, "Be home to eat—
Breakfast and dinner; the rest is your beat."
So I took her word and slept on the sand,
Stars as my ceiling, sea in my hand.

The world opened up like a windowpane,
A truth my grandparents tried to explain:
"You can be anyone, anywhere too,"
And suddenly, wildly, I knew it was true.

We danced on buses, sang Beatles out loud,
Traveled to London, felt young and proud.
Wrote postcards in Rome with gelato-stained fingers,
The scent of adventure still sweetly lingers.

Jenny and I shared secrets at night,
Curled in our room, her mood feather-light.
We spoke of the future in flickering tones,
Of cities, and lovers, and lives of our own.

But life so often doesn't play fair.
At twenty-one, she vanished into thin air.
And yet she still lingers in sunsets and songs,
In the South of France, where her heart belongs.

On her fortieth, I returned once more,
Knocked on the sun-painted French front door.
Took my French family out to dine,
Raised a glass to that friend of mine.

Full circle spun in golden grace,
In every memory, I saw her face.
Though her years were few, they stretched so wide—
A lifetime lived with me by her side.

Now I walk with a worldly stride,
A woman shaped by oceans and tide.
Because once, at sixteen, I dared to roam—
And found in the world a second home.

finding home

Before her own children filled her days,
She journeyed to Africa, to see a new way.
The promise of safaris, nature's wide sights,
But first—a village, where truths came to light.

The jeep rattled on streets worn thin,
A world of struggle, chaos within.
Sounds of life, and perhaps of fear,
The echo of gunfire distant, unclear.

Her heart began to race, her breath turned tight,
Doubt crept in, stealing the light.
She said nothing, not even to her husband near,
Ashamed of her trembling, ashamed of her fear.

Stepping out, her boot met a puddle's embrace,
A cold, muddy welcome to this unfamiliar place.
She froze in her doubt, her regret running deep,
When a sound broke the silence, pulling her steep.

Children came running, laughter in tow,
Tiny bare feet on the ground below.
One small boy, with eyes so wide,
Locked onto hers, the world aside.

Without a word, he reached for her hand,
A gesture of trust she didn't understand.
He pulled her forward, toward a fading home,
Where his dying mother waited in the unknown.

In that moment, her fear slipped away,
Replaced by a calm she couldn't betray.
His touch, his gaze, spoke loud and clear,
A truth she'd sought but hadn't been near.

This was the reason, the path, the start,
A shift, a calling, deep in her heart.
She was ready now, the answer she'd missed,
To love, to nurture, to exist.

This world wasn't fear; it wasn't regret.
It was a place where her soul had been met.
In the eyes of a child, she found her truth,
The next step of her life, her unshaken proof.

the simplicity of you

It came so fast, the moment arrived,
An hour from water breaking to life.
The rush, the noise, the world a blur,
Until you were placed, soft and sure.

On my chest, you rested small and still,
And all at once, the world bent to my will.
The choices once tangled, the questions unclear,
Melted away with you lying here.

No more drama, no endless debate,
You brought focus; you quieted fate.
A clarity I'd yearned for, long and true,
Now lived in the simplicity of you.

Without a family left to call mine,
You healed the space with purpose divine.
You weren't just my child, my beautiful boy;
You were the answer, the root of my joy.

In the nights, I rocked you, my hands in tune,
To the rhythm of love under a silver moon.
My palm would linger on your neck's soft skin,
A silent bond where words couldn't begin.

And one day, as I cradled you tight,
Older now, yet still my light,
You reached around with a tender grace,
And rubbed the same spot, the very same place.

In that touch, I felt it all,
The unspoken link, unshaken, tall.
You knew me as deeply as I knew you,
Our connection eternal, simple, and true.

You gave me focus; you gave me peace,
A love that grows, that will never cease.
With you, my son, my life made whole,
You are the center, the depth of my soul.

bound by love

I brought you home, my second light,
A daughter born in a world so bright.
Your brother, a mere two years older,
Waited, his heart now drawing you closer.
A tiny crib, a tender gaze.
Your hand in his, his eyes so wide,
As if he'd found his purpose inside.

From that first touch, a connection was made,
A love so pure, it couldn't fade.
He cared for you, so gentle, so true,
Every step, he carried you through.

In toddler years, his care so deep,
He held you close, your trust to keep.
I'd gently say, "Let her try on her own.
She'll grow her wings; she's not alone."

Yet still, his heart would always defend,
You weren't just his sister—you were his best friend.
Through childhood games and laughter's song,
You grew together, your friendship so strong.

I remember the day, your first little fight,
Nine and eleven, voices raised in spite.
I stopped you both, and softly said,
"Listen to the words in your head.

"One day, I won't be here to guide,
But you'll have each other, side by side.
Count on each other, hold this love true,
Your history is something no one else knew."

I saw in your eyes, the lesson take hold,
Tears brimming as the moment told.
You hugged each other, a silent vow,
A promise that lives in your hearts even now.

And since that day, through every storm,
You've found your way back to the warm.
Arguments rare, and quickly resolved,
A love that evolves but stays involved.

Now I watch you, grown and free,
Two halves of a sacred family tree.
The love you share, unbroken, divine,
A gift I treasure, forever mine.

For siblings are blessings, a treasure so rare,
And you've shown me love beyond compare.
From the crib to now,
You've known what I didn't always know.

my miracle

My daughter had been a dancer, swift and strong,
Kicking in rhythm, her cadence a song.
But one day her movements slowed to a hum,
A quiet signal of what was to come.

A test, a room, a doctor's firm gaze,
"You're having this baby early . . . today?"
The words hung heavy, but calm I stayed,
Called a sitter for my son, her day's plans remade.

My husband rushed home, just off the plane,
The world spun fast, yet I felt no strain.
In the blur of lights, the sterile air,
My daughter was born, fragile but rare.

Pink and strong, though less than three pounds,
Her spirit defied the hospital grounds.
The doctor whispered, "A miraculous day—
Tomorrow's path wouldn't look this way."

The words reached me, but they didn't take hold,
My focus was clear: to be steady, to be bold.
For hours they tested, for hours I prayed,
And in the end, the fears put at bay.

The doctor returned, his face soft with grace,
"Do you remember the words I placed?
Your instincts spoke when mine were dim—
Honey, you saved her. You listened to them."

The doctor confessed his tears, his humbling sight,
Of how my courage lit the night.
A trust in myself, a new mother's will,
A knowledge so deep, unbroken still.

And so, with my daughter, I found my stride,
No fear, no doubt, no need to hide.
Though born too soon, her spirit was vast,
A miracle rooted in love steadfast.

The bond that we share, unshaken, divine,
A thread unbreakable, a sacred line.
For in my arms, I held much more—
A life, a strength, a love to adore.

This daughter, a miracle, fierce and true,
Her spirit unyielding, her heart brand-new.
And the mother, now fearless, walks each day,
Knowing love's power lights the way.

a little spitfire

Six weeks early, my world held its breath,
As you came too soon, so close to the edge.
Tiny and fragile, in the NICU's light,
I watched over you through the long sleepless nights.

I'd pump my milk, my offering of love,
A mother's gift, sent with prayers above.
Through a feeding tube, they'd nurture you, so small,
While I'd run back home to answer your brother's call.

Back and forth, my days a blur,
Half with him, half with her.
I'd ask the nurses, my heart in doubt,
"Will she thrive? Will she make it out?"

They'd smile, their voices calm and pure,
"Honey, you've got a spitfire for sure.
She's got fight in her; she's fierce; she's strong;
She'll be just fine; she's where she belongs."

And they were right—you grew, you thrived,
Every ounce a triumph, every day alive.
Your birth story, you've always known,
A tale of courage, all your own.

At thirteen, with friends gathered near,
You asked me to tell it again, loud and clear.
So I spoke of those days, the worry, the strife,
The miracle of your early life.

Tears streamed as you listened, your heart so wide.
"Oh, Mommy, I get it," you softly cried.
"I understand now how lucky I am,
How close I came to a different plan."

And in that moment, I saw, you see,
The strength you carried, the fire, the key.
Born too soon, but never too weak,
A spitfire spirit, unbroken, unique.

You are my miracle, my proof of grace,
A daughter who fought for her rightful place.
And as I watch you, so bold, so free,
I thank the stars for giving you to me.

the space between us

The teenage years, a stormy sea,
A dance of love and uncertainty.
Her daughter pulled, the mother held tight,
A battle of wills in the dead of night.

The words exchanged, the doors that closed,
A bond once clear, now juxtaposed.
The mother, aching, had to let go,
To trust her daughter's path, though she didn't yet know.

She surrendered her grip, her need to control,
Hoping her love still tethered her soul.
Silent prayers filled the empty space,
Trusting time to restore their grace.

And then, like dawn breaking after the storm,
The daughter returned, her heart newly warm.
She saw the sacrifice, the quiet pain,
Her mother's love, unspoken, plain.

Now college years bring a tender bloom,
Daily calls to light up the room.
Mother-daughter weekends, laughter anew,
A friendship forged, steadfast and true.

Through need and joy, the daughter now sees,
The depth of her mother's heart, her pleas.
For in her mother, she's found her guide,
A love so deep, it can't be denied.

They're best friends now, a bond so rare,
Built on trust, on space, on care.
The mother, fulfilled, her heart alight,
For this was the dream she held so tight.

And the daughter, too, feels love so vast,
Rooted in struggles that didn't last.
For through the storms, they both have grown,
A bond unshaken, forever their own.

And so, they walk this life as one,
Through every challenge, every sun.
A mother's love, a daughter's grace,
Forever held in that sacred space.

hope, the tenth

It began with a question, a simple idea,
Two children at home, ages near.
A thought of a dog, a bond to unfold,
A companion to love, a heart to hold.

In Lake Tahoe's light, fate wrote its song,
A chance meeting where hearts belonged.
A couple spoke of eleven pups, nine already given away,
So I asked for the tenth, my decision not to sway.

Weeks later, we journeyed, anticipation high,
To meet the small wonder who'd catch our eye.
A chocolate-brown Labradoodle, soft and bright,
Her blue eyes shifting with nature's light.

From blue to green, then a human-like hue,
Her gaze seemed to know the world we knew.
We named her Hope, a fitting call,
For she brought a new joy that lifted us all.

With children at thirteen and eleven, Hope grew,
A family pet, loyal and true.
Through games in the yard and snuggles at night,
Her love was constant, her presence light.

But as children do, they grew and they soared,
Off to universities, new lives explored.
And I, now alone, with dreams to expand,
Found my path in Italy, a beautiful land.

Hope came with me, as steadfast as ever,
With an Italian passport, bound by endeavor.
On every plane, in every new place,
Her wagging tail brought a sense of grace.

From Tuscan hills to coastal views,
Hope walked beside me, steady and true.
A companion, a guardian, a soul so near,
Her silent love wiped away any fear.

For in her eyes, I found my calm,
A reminder of home, a soothing balm.
She cared for me, as I did for her,
A bond unbroken, steadfast and pure.

Now, years have passed, and she's still by my side,
Through life's great journeys, with love as our guide.
For an animal's love is a gift so rare,
A partnership sacred, beyond compare.

Hope was the tenth, the question's reply,
The joy that began when she caught our eye.
She's more than a pet; she's family and friend,
A story of love that will never end.

a good decision

I tried for years to bridge the divide,
To mend the wounds, to let love abide.
But patterns persisted, unchanged, unfair,
A mother's love that was never quite there.

There was no trust, only distance disguised,
Held back by a husband's protective guise.
When he was gone, her anger unfurled,
And I stood my ground to shield my world.

When I told them the truth, my voice was calm,
Shielding my hurt, my quiet psalm.
My son, just nine, his head hung low,
Tears in his eyes, emotions to show.

"It's okay, buddy, we have so much love,
From family, from friends, from heaven above."
But his words cut deep, so wise, so true,
"I'm not crying for me, Mommy; I'm crying for you.

"If she didn't love you the way you love us,
Then walking away is an act of trust.
A good decision, Mommy, good decision made,
To break the cycle, let the shadows fade."

In that moment, my heart both broke and healed,
A child's wisdom, a truth revealed.
His words became the strength I needed,
A validation for which my heart had pleaded.

To this day, I hold that truth close,
A guiding star in the life I chose.
For I'm the mother I never had,
Loving my children through the good and the bad.

My son's maturity, his tender grace,
A reflection of love I put in place.
And though estranged from the mother I knew,
I built a family that's whole and true.

For cycles break when courage is found,
When love is given, whole and unbound.
And in my children, I see my story,
A legacy of love, my truest glory.

a playful tug-a-tumble

In line for basketball, papers in hand,
Her son stood waiting, quiet and grand.
Her daughter, six, with energy wild,
Ran back and forth, her joyful child.

She'd grab her mom, giggling with glee,
Hugging her thighs where she could reach, you see.
The line began to smile and stare,
At the sweet little girl with her carefree flair.

But then it happened, a playful tug,
Her little hands caught on fabric snug.
In one swift motion, the skirt gave way,
At her mother's ankles it decided to stay.

Gasps and laughter rippled the line,
The mom froze briefly, pretending all was fine.
With a quick bend down, her head out of sight,
She yanked her skirt back up to its height.

The daughter just giggled, clueless and free,
While her brother turned red, wishing not to see.
The counter clerk hid a grin behind a hand,
As the mom stood tall, trying to withstand.

Embarrassed? Yes, but her heart held cheer,
For moments like this are fleeting, yet dear.
Kids bring chaos, and laughter too,
Even when they reveal more than they're due.

She laughed it off as the line moved along,
Knowing these days don't last for long.
For in every mishap, in every small mess,
Lives the joy of parenting's sweet, funny stress.

the asking

I used to speak in hints,
in softened tones,
in wishes made quiet enough
not to echo back unmet.
Because when I was young,
the asking felt dangerous.
Not for toys or trinkets—
but for tenderness,
for presence,
for someone to look at me
and really see.
I learned young
that silence was safer
than the ache of asking
and hearing nothing in return.
But love came in through the cracks—
my grandparents,
their hands and time,
their everyday,

showed me what it looked like
to be wanted
without having to beg.
Still, asking has been a lesson
learned slow.
Especially as a woman—
where we're trained to negotiate in nuance,
to offer disclaimers with our dreams,
to smile while shrinking.
Men don't flinch when they ask.
Not in business.
Not in love.
They state.
They expect.
And I admire that.
There's no shame in the clean lines
of a clear desire.
So now,
I practice.
I name.
I ask.
Not with apology,
but with presence.
With the understanding
that no one can give me what I need
if I won't let them see it.
Life keeps rising to meet me
the more I ask.
And I keep discovering
that knowing what I want
isn't selfish—
it's sacred.
The more I speak it,
the more I live it.

And the more I live it,
the more I know
that my voice
was never the problem.

part 3
finding purpose in creativity, travel, and career

the flow of a dream

Three years, three homes, built with care,
Each one a vision, a story to share.
Luxury crafted with a personal touch,
A dream unfolding, a life that's lush.

Press comes calling, articles told,
Of a woman whose courage turns dreams into gold.
Interviews air; her story takes flight,
A bigger project now in sight.

An investment hotel, a grander design,
A testament to years spent redefining the line.
For in these builds, she begins to see
Her true self rooted in creativity.

Corporate paths have shaped her days,
But her heart beats loud in other ways.
Design and detail, the soul of her art,
Each space creates a piece of her heart.

And through it all, the flow remains clear,
Parenting, puppies, Palm Springs, so dear.
The first house bought, a start to it all,
A sanctuary where her dreams stand tall.

The last in Italy, where pasta is shared,
A land of beauty, a life repaired.
Her kids by her side, her dog at her feet,
A joy-filled rhythm, steady and sweet.

From desert sands to Puglia skies,
Her journey expands, her spirit flies.
A creative life, a story untold,
A future bright, a dream of gold.

For it's not just the homes, the press, or the name,
But the love she's poured into every frame.
A life defined by the flow she's found,
A woman whose roots are in solid ground.

code and soul

It began where the wires first whispered awake,
In a valley where light bloomed from circuit and stake.
I stood at the edge where the pixels first played,
Built the web's first doors, carved code in the shade.

An ad shop with vision, no rules to obey,
We sold Estée Lauder their first web page,
On IPO roadshows with stars in our stride,
The pulse of the market—a thrilling tide.

Then New York called with its neon and might,
I rose up Madison, chasing the light,
Led teams through the static, the swirl, and the spin,
Bringing brands to the screen from deep within.

The world stretched open—Tokyo, Rome,
With nothing but signals to carry me home.
We rewired medicine, gave doctors new eyes,
Put charts in their palms, watched healing digitize.

The apps in pockets and voices in air,
We shaped how the world found what wasn't there.
User experience—now intelligence too,
Designing the future from an ever-shifting view.

Then children arrived, like soft, sacred signs,
So I paused for their mornings, their fingers in mine.
Between playgrounds and meetings, I found a new way,
To honor both wonder and working each day.

Now I partially live where olives and ocean collide,
Split time between sunsets, let values decide.
Grateful, still, for the arc of it all—
The rise and the reach, the thrill and the fall.

Yet here in the hum of a bright, buzzing age,
I see what we've built can both nurture and cage.
The scroll never ends, the hearts grow thin—
And I wonder sometimes what we've invited in.

So I walk with intent, plant seeds that are true,
Have raised children with conscience in all that they do.
And design, still, with care—my quiet reply:
Let this all serve the soul, not just catch the eye.

the trails we keep

Rachel grew up in Michigan, me in the sun,
California days where life had begun.
Midwest kindness met West Coast fire,
A friendship built on shared desire—
To raise our kids, to laugh, to grieve,
To hold each other when it was time to leave.

We've moved homes, moved lives, watched years unfold,
Through loss and love, both quiet and bold.
Parents passing, children grown,
Parties where joy and laughter were sewn.
Tears of pride, tears of pain,
Talking through storms, dancing in rain.

But always, our solace was found on the trail,
With Blue and Hope, tails wagging, no fail.
Hikes through the hills, just dogs and us two,
Sorting life's chaos, finding what's true.

The Bay was our anchor, a chapter we shared,
We both moved on, but memories flared.
Back to our favorite hotel we'd go,
Not for the city, but for what we know—
The walks, the talks, the ties that remain,
A place where nostalgia softens the pain.

Now there's no reason to return,
No ties to loosen, no bridges to burn.
But we'll keep meeting, in one place or another,
Bound by a friendship like no other.

For Blue and Hope once led the way,
And their spirit lingers in every day.
Through laughter, tears, and life's great tide,
We'll keep this bond, forever our guide.

elegant and the echo

In Italy for work, I carried the weight,
Of a friend now gone, stolen by fate.
A race car driver, bold and free,
Rome's streets once echoed his energy.

His loss was fresh, his spirit missed,
But I pushed through, though shadows persist.
I worked, I wandered, sought something bright,
A way to feel whole in the fading light.

North I went, a date gone astray,
An ending before it began that day.
So I walked to find solace, my dog in tow,
Through Monza Park, where soft winds blow.

The stables appeared, their doors ajar,
A world of quiet beneath each star.
I toured the horses, their beauty untamed,
Touching and snuggling, learning each name.

And then, in the corner, my eyes caught his,
A white horse, still, with a presence that is.
I moved through the others, but he drew me near,
His gaze was a whisper only I could hear.

When I reached him, my heart slowed its pace,
I stroked his mane, and time left no trace.
We lingered together, a bond so new,
An unspoken connection, deep and true.

As I turned to go, he knocked his hoof,
A sound that echoed, gentle yet aloof.
The workers watched, their voices low,
"That horse is sad, you know.

"Elegant, his name, he's known despair,
But for you, he stirred; that's rare."
I paused, reluctant to part,
For Elegant had touched the core of my heart.

Hey hey hey. We left the stables, my dog by my side,
But questions lingered, impossible to hide.
I wandered the park, lost in thought,
And stumbled upon what fate had brought.

A curve in the road, a familiar ring,
The Formula One track, where engines sing.
My friend, the driver, flashed through my mind—
Was this his message, subtle yet kind?

Through Elegant's gaze and the knock on the door,
Was he telling me he's with me once more?
A moment of love, a bridge through the veil,
In a park in Monza, a whispered tale.

I carried the thought, both heavy and light,
That connections persist, unseen in their might.
Elegant, the horse, with sadness and grace,
Became the reflection of my friend's embrace.

the parisi table

In Ostuni's light, where the olive trees sway,
We met the Parisi family one sunlit day.
Focaccia and pasta, hands in the dough,
A feast of tradition, where love would grow.

My kids were young, their laughter sweet,
Running and playing, flour on their feet.
The Parisis embraced us, their home so wide,
In a family's warmth we couldn't hide.

Around the table, stories were told,
Of generations past, of bread and gold.
Their joy was simple, their bond so true,
A reflection of dreams I longed to pursue.

It was then I saw the path I'd take,
A legacy for my children, a life I'd make.
A home in Italy, where hearts could meet,
Where laughter and love would fill every seat.

Over the years, I'd return to this place,
With friends who'd marvel at the Parisi grace.
Each visit a spark, a reminder anew,
Of the vision I carried, the life I'd pursue.

Now, as I stand in my own Italian sun,
I see that the dream and the work are one.
The legacy I yearned for, the life I'd planned,
Has grown from the seeds I held in my hand.

The Parisis taught me that community's art
Is opening your home and sharing your heart.
Though my journey is mine, the spirit is shared,
A life of connection, of love deeply cared.

This table I've built, these homes I create,
Are reflections of joy, of bending fate.
From Ostuni's kitchen to my own space,
I've learned that dreams begin with grace.

For in the dough, the laughter, the light,
I found my purpose, my guiding sight.
And as I reflect on the journey I've known,
I realize I'm living the legacy I've sown.

wheels of discovery

A bus full of teenagers, hearts open wide,
On French roads winding, with dreams as their guide.
Weekends spent chasing the sun and the sea,
Through France, Italy, and England's green spree.

Laughter-filled air, the hum of the ride,
Voices that harmonized, worlds would collide.
Songs sung loudly, off-key but sincere,
As the journey ahead erased every fear.

On the Riviera, they slept by the tide,
Stars overhead, the ocean their guide.
The girls met boys, Hyde Park their stage,
Cigarettes shared, a youthful page.

Wine sipped awkwardly, laughter untamed,
Their first taste of freedom, no guilt, no shame.
The meals, the markets, the baguettes and cheese,
The clink of glasses, the Mediterranean breeze.

Each moment a lesson, though none could yet see,
How the world's vastness shapes who you'll be.
For in the echoes of laughter and song,
They were learning that life is a dance, a throng.

The choices they'd make, the paths they'd take,
Were molded by beaches, by trains, by lakes.
The world they discovered in those fleeting days,
Would guide them through life in mysterious ways.

Now as adults, they look back and smile,
At the bus rides, the love, the mile upon mile.
For those trips were more than a youthful spree,
They were windows to life, to possibility.

The world felt bigger, the future more clear,
Through laughter, adventure, and facing their fear.
And though time has scattered them far and wide,
The bond of that bus still burns inside.

It whispers of freedom, of joy, of the start,
Of the lessons of youth that still guide the heart.
And in quiet moments, they close their eyes,
Hearing the songs under foreign skies.

the cliff's edge

I stood at the edge, the world below,
My heart racing fast, my courage running slow.
A jungle stretched far, the ocean in sight,
But fear gripped me tight on that towering height.

The guide stood near, calm and composed.
"You must run," he said, "to where the line goes."
My feet shuffled forward, then froze in place,
The fear painted clear on my pale face.

"Can you push me?" I asked, my voice a plea,
But he shook his head. "That's not up to me.
It has to be you, your choice to make,
To leap off this cliff, the courage to take."

Once, twice, I tried, my legs betrayed,
Stopping short where the leap was made.
I'd step back, negotiate, try to delay,
But the beauty ahead still called me to stay.

On the third attempt, I faltered again,
But this time, the guide leaned in just then.
A gentle shove, a nudge so slight,
And I soared into the open light.

The wind kissed my face, my fear fell away,
The jungle below a vibrant display.
The ocean beyond, endless and blue,
A world so alive came into view.

My partner waited on the other side,
Arms outstretched, a beacon of pride.
And in that moment, clarity came,
How sometimes we all need help just the same.

A little push, a guiding hand,
To take us farther than we had planned.
The beauty we find, the freedom we feel,
When we face our fears and let life reveal.

I touched down safely, my heart now light,
The cliff behind me, no longer in sight.
For in that leap, I found my way,
A brighter journey, a brighter day.

the journey within

She liked wandering alone in her early years,
Her compass guided by dreams, not fears.
From bustling streets to the quiet unknown,
Her footsteps marked paths she claimed as her own.

Yet solitude, her trusted friend,
Brings moments of wonder, but doesn't pretend.
For loneliness lingers, soft and unkind,
A shadow that travels in the back of her mind.

One train ride through Salzburg, the world painted white,
Mountains embraced by the softest light.
The window framed beauty too grand to contain,
And yet tears fell like the softest rain.

No one beside her to share the view,
No voice to echo, "I see it too."
In that fleeting ache, her heart turned to stone,
A reminder of journeys often made alone.

But the very next day, in Vienna's embrace,
The streets were alive, a vibrant place.
She stood in the center, no soul in sight,
Yet her heart was alight with quiet might.

No one knew where she was that day,
No map to follow, no roles to play.
For a moment, the world was solely hers,
A life unbound by the crowd's constant murmurs.

And so she learned, as travelers do,
That loneliness whispers, but strength breaks through.
One day sorrow, the next, a flame,
Both part of the journey, both the same.

a journey of creation

She once built dreams through meetings and minds,
Where clients and creatives shaped future designs.
A career that shimmered, with tech so vast,
Yet life whispered softly, "This moment won't last."

When children arrived, her world rearranged,
Priorities shifted, her pace exchanged.
She poured herself into their tiny days,
Finding joy in their laughter, their curious gaze.

Her creativity bloomed in a different light,
Crafting a home, making their world bright.
Each milestone cherished, each moment divine,
Her heart content in love's design.

But as they grew, so did her call,
To show them strength, to rise from it all.
To prove independence, to dream once more,
She stepped back through the corporate door.

Yet the clock ticked on, her soul took a turn,
For deeper meaning she started to yearn.
She left behind the corporate grind,
Seeking a purpose more intertwined.

In Italy's hills, she found her art,
Building spaces that spoke to the heart.
Luxury homes, but more than a stay,
A haven for travelers who'd lost their way.

Her work became her legacy's thread,
Honoring her family, the life she led.
For in every stone and every view,
Was the story of strength, of dreams renewed.

A woman of vision, of courage and grace,
She built not just homes, but a healing space.
In her children's eyes, she sees it clear,
The path she forges will always endear.

the day fate wrapped us together

It was my fiftieth, a change of course,
A deal fell through, but life found its force.
With my kids by my side, we sought the sun,
To Positano's shores where the day had begun.

On a boat to a beach, just a casual ride,
Lauren and Becca sat nearby, wide-eyed.
A comment was made, so simple, so light,
"Your wrap is stunning," Lauren said, a-bright.

By the end of the day, they'd joined our spree,
Swimming with my kids, laughing carefree.
On the deck we shared stories, wine in hand,
Strangers turned friends by fate's quiet command.

Now, years have passed, and the bond holds true,
Paris, Mexico, Italy too.
Trips we've taken, memories we've spun,
Moments of joy under every sun.

They teach me my kids' unspoken view,
I guide them to see what parents once knew.
In their mid-thirties, they stand like me,
Single, strong, and wild, yet free.

A cover-up sparked what words can't define,
A friendship as rare as the Amalfi coastline.
What began with a comment, so casual, so small,
Became one of life's greatest gifts of all.

standing ovation

We dreamed of change, a bold new way,
to heal the gaps where systems fray.
The first of its kind—a record reborn,
to bridge the care where trust was torn.

A tool for patients, a voice, a guide,
to own their records, to stand with pride.
A bridge for doctors, a clearer view,
A way to heal the old and new.

The stage was set; the hall was wide,
A world of doctors side by side.
The screen lit up, the promise near,
and every heart leaned in to hear.

When words gave way to what we'd made,
The room erupted, dreams displayed.
A standing cheer, a roaring spark—
A moment carved to leave its mark.

The client smiled; the world had seen,
The birth of something once just a dream.
From thought to form, from plan to pride,
A future opened, unified.

And in that moment, joy took flight,
A lasting glow, a shared delight.
For what we built will long remain—
A shift in care, a lasting gain.

the shape of a dream

I once dreamed of Italy, and then I arrived,
In the heart of Puglia, where the old trees thrive.
A home in Valle d'Itria, stone and sky,
With golden oil and guests passing by.

The artists, the thinkers, the ones who create,
Gathered in beauty—what a twist of fate.
Success in the fields, joy in the air,
Yet in quiet moments, I felt something rare.

At fifty-five, I stood so strong,
Yet longing for love, for where I belong.
This house was a chapter, but not the whole book,
So I turned the page, took a second look.

I let the house go, with grace, with ease,
Not my forever—just the first breeze.
And then I chose, not just one, but two,
A vision expanding, a dream breaking through.

First, a palazzo, close to the sea,
A gift for my children, a piece of me.
Their names on its walls, its history made,
A place for our roots, where memories stay.

Then onto the land, where the wild vines grow,
A new kind of dream, a stage set to show—
A boutique retreat, for those who create,
A vineyard, a haven, a place to celebrate.

Art on the walls, wine in the glass,
Sustainable feasts, where time moves slow, not fast.
A home for expression, for those drawn near,
A sanctuary pulsing with laughter and cheer.

And in this space, as walls were raised,
Poetry found me in quiet days.
The solitude taught me, the whispers grew,
The truth of my path became something new.

Some cheered, some doubted, some faded away,
Yet I kept building, come what may.
Because the dream was bigger than I first knew,
One part for my children, one for the world too.

A legacy now, not just of stone,
But of vision, of love, of seeds that are sown.
A tribute to those who came before,
And a future that sings forevermore.

part 4

love and letting go

a bond divided

We built a family once, with hands intertwined,
Joyous days of my life, the moments defined.
The day they were born, our hearts held tight,
A fleeting glimpse of love's true light.

But time unraveled what we thought was strong,
Pain buried deep, where we both went wrong.
And though the marriage faded, I believed,
We could co-parent, their lives interweaved.

Yet you turned away, held tightly to pride,
Unable to put the hurt aside.
I don't want you back, that's never been true,
But I thought for them, we'd find something new.

For seventeen years, I've carried the weight,
Of confusion, of sorrow, of this fractured state.
You've remarried, moved on, built a life,
But still, our children feel the strife.

Why couldn't you see the gift we were given?
Two souls, their love so purely driven.
Why couldn't we celebrate what they became,
Instead of letting the hurt stake its claim?

The pain is mine, but theirs is worse,
A wound unspoken, a silent curse.
For in the tug-of-war, they stand between,
The broken bond, the unseen scene.

Yet even through this, my heart remains,
Focused on them, through joy and pain.
The day they were born, my world stood still,
A moment of love that time couldn't kill.

And though we can't share in that joy anew,
I'll cherish it, even without you.
For their laughter, their love, their light so free,
Is the only connection that binds you and me.

I've learned to accept what I can't amend,
But I still grieve what we couldn't transcend.
Not for us, but for what they deserved,
A love united, their peace preserved.

the quiet cage

She lived in a house, but it wasn't a home,
A place where her heart was left to roam.
He smiled in the daylight, played his part,
But at night, he ruled the silence, the dark.

He cared for control, not her gentle needs,
Preyed on her doubts, on her deepest pleads.
When cracks appeared, he chose to defend,
Not their love—but the power he refused to bend.

His words were sharp, his gaze a weight,
Belittling her dreams, sealing her fate.
When she sought comfort, he left her alone,
A queen dethroned, in a kingdom of stone.

Familiar it was, this quiet despair,
A mirror of pain she'd learned to bear.
Not as cruel as the past, but close enough,
The echoes of hurt made the present seem tough.

And so she stayed, caught in the bind,
Of love and fear, of heart and mind.
For even in pain, there's a pull to remain
Where the chaos feels steady, despite the strain.

But this story is common, its shadows vast,
A silence shared by too many cast.
It's vital to speak; to break the spell,
To lift the veil where so many dwell.

For love is not power, nor fear, nor control.
It's freedom, compassion, the healing of souls.
To those who are trapped, your voice is your key—
Speak your truth, and set yourself free.

the mask

She smiles in the mirror, perfect and poised,
A picture of grace, rehearsed in the noise.
Lipstick flawless, eyes so bright,
A practiced glow in the softest light.

To the world, she's warmth, a gentle hand,
A dream of love, so carefully planned.
She speaks in tones so sugar-sweet,
A melody spun for all she meets.

But beneath the charm, behind the scene,
She counts the ways this life's unseen.
Not a path she'd carve, not a dream she drew,
Yet here she stands in borrowed shoes.

She saw the weight, the extra thread,
A tangled life, a past unsaid.
Not woven in, not part of her plan,
A love that asked for more than one hand.

She measured the cost; she named the toll,
Not love in full, but love on hold.
An inconvenience, not a prize,
A burden masked behind her eyes.

Yet love, when weighed, becomes a debt,
A house half-built, a deep regret.
And children feel what's left unsaid,
A shadow cast where warmth once spread.

They learned too young what coldness breeds,
How love withdrawn still leaves its seeds.
A silent wound, a heavy air,
A home that bent beneath her stare.

And all the while, she played her part,
Yet never let them touch her heart.
She stayed, but distant, near yet far,
A presence felt, but never warm.

Her love was measured, thin and frayed,
A hollow space that never swayed.
She did not leave, yet just the same,
The emptiness still bore her name.

first love, forever fond

They met in the youth of high school days,
A love that blossomed in innocent ways.
He played basketball; she cheered in the stands,
A bond that grew with gentle hands.

His family welcomed her into its fold,
Kindness and trust, a love to behold.
Late nights at each other's homes they'd stay,
Building memories that wouldn't fade away.

Then illness came, casting a shadow near,
But she stayed by his side, calm and sincere.
Wheeling him through halls, her heart never swayed,
A love that cared, a love that stayed.

Four years together, no drama, no fight,
Just life pulling them in separate flights.
They parted as friends, no bitterness found,
Just a quiet goodbye, their love still profound.

Years passed by, as life often does,
Marriage and heartbreak, the push and the buzz.
In the world of dating, she came to know,
Some loves aren't as pure as the one long ago.

And then one day, on a screen she spied,
His mother, now eighty, her pride amplified.
A comment she left, a piece of her past,
The kindness she showed, how it seemed to last.

The mother replied, her words like a gift,
A validation that caused her heart to lift.
"We remember you well, the girl so kind,
A piece of our hearts you've left behind."

Her high school sweetheart, his wife by his side,
Both hearted the post, no reason to hide.
No jealousy, no pain, just grace displayed,
A kindness that time and love had made.

In that moment, the years fell away,
She saw herself in a brighter way.
Her love had mattered; her care was true,
A first love cherished, her heart anew.

For in this world, where love feels rare,
A memory can remind you of what's still there.
The kindness we give, the love we show,
Are threads that weave through lives we know.

still waiting

At fifty-five, she stands so strong,
Her life a melody, a well-worn song.
Divorced, grown kids, her chapter brand-new,
Happy, independent, her sky bright and blue.

She's tasted love, its sweet, fleeting kiss,
Felt its warmth and its weight, its moments of bliss.
Some loves were bright, others turned gray,
Lessons learned on the winding way.

But still, she wonders, deep in her heart,
If that one true love will ever start.
The kind that stays, that roots and grows,
That whispers softly, that deeply knows.

Complicated feelings, they ebb and flow,
A mix of patience and the ache to know.
When will it happen? And where will it be?
Is love still waiting somewhere for me?

She's open, she says, ready to find,
A partner who'll match her independent mind.
Yet doubts creep in, soft as a breeze;
Can love still surprise her, still bring her to her knees?

She's lived enough to know her worth,
To find joy in solitude, in life's rebirth.
But the longing remains, a quiet refrain,
A hope she's carried through pleasure and pain.

And so she moves forward, her heart open wide,
Curious about what the future will provide.
For love is a mystery, a patient friend,
Arriving when ready, not knowing the end.

Until that day, she'll live as she must,
With strength in her stride and faith in her trust.
For she knows her own story, her beauty, her fire,
And true love, when it comes, will only inspire.

the love of family

They were never quite sisters, not by name,
Bound by a chapter that ended the same.
Her mother, her father, a fleeting pair,
But what remained was a bond so rare.

Through years apart, their lives would stray,
Yet the thread between them never gave way.
In New York's hum, when illness grew near,
The older stood steady, a force to cheer.

Her care was quiet, her presence strong,
A reminder that love doesn't need to belong.
It simply exists, a steady light,
A harbor of warmth in the coldest night.

Years passed, and tables turned,
The older one's heart now scarred and burned.
A divorce, a business, the weight of despair,
The younger stepped in, her love laid bare.

Though distance lingered, and calls grew few,
Their actions spoke louder than words could do.
When needed most, they'd always show,
A family forged where blood doesn't flow.

For neither had much family to claim,
But they built their own, without need for a name.
Through trials and triumphs, laughter and tears,
They proved that love transcends the years.

Now they stand, apart yet near,
Two hearts that hold each other dear.
Though their lives may wander, their roots remain,
A bond unbroken by loss or pain.

For family is not just whom we're born to,
It's who stays steady when skies aren't blue.
And in their love, they've come to see,
They've built their own kind of family.

rest easy, diane

I knew Diane for twenty-five years.
Time made us close; life brought us near.
We met through brothers, young and free,
Building lives and families, as it was meant to be.

Yet early days weren't always kind;
Challenges lingered, harmony hard to find.
Friendly moments came, but drifted away;
Something between us kept pulling astray.

Then life, as it does, brought change unforeseen,
I was single with children at just five and three.
Diane divorced, and reached out to me.
"Let's meet," she said, "and let our kids be."

Reluctant, I agreed, unsure in my heart.
Could we rebuild what was broken apart?
She arrived with joy, her natural light,
While I approached with cautious might.

But love for our children built a bridge anew,
Honesty and care pulled us through.
We spoke of the past, and chose a new way,
For us, and our children, to grow and stay.

What we created, I'll always hold dear,
A bond of depth, devotion, and cheer.
We raised our children, side by side,
Proving family's form need not be tied.

Beyond the chats of work and design,
It's the time with the kids that stands in my mind.
Holidays, dinners, the simplest things,
The laughter and love true friendship brings.

She marveled at Sydney, her grace, her fire,
Her intellect, courage, and dreams that inspire.
"Syd will slay it," she'd always say,
"The world is hers in every way."

And KK, her heart, her person, her pride,
An artist, a dancer, a strength she'd confide.
She worried, she loved, but always knew,
Your focus and independence would guide you through.

In her final days, you gave her care,
Love unconditional, a bond so rare.
She taught you well; she saw it shine,
In your courage, your hearts, your love divine.

Diane, you lived with purpose and grace,
A friend, a mother, a light in this space.
In those final hours, your hand touched mine,
And I whispered softly, "It's your time."

But know this, my friend, your girls are not alone,
In their hearts and ours, your love is home.
We'll hold them close, as you held us all,
Through life's triumphs and every fall.

Rest easy, Diane; your love remains,
A legacy bright through joys and pains.
And in time, as we mend what's torn,
We'll reunite where love is reborn.

a dream, misunderstood

We met over coffee, her presence strong,
A woman I'd known and admired so long.
Independent, bold, she'd carved her way,
A mirror, I thought, to who I am today.

She asked of Italy, my newest pride,
Of homes I'd built, where dreams abide.
Then her question came to my dismay,
"Was it a man who brought you that way?"

I paused, surprised, a moment to think,
How easily assumptions form and sink.
"No," I said, "it's a dream long sown,
A legacy for my kids, all my own.

"I'm Italian; my roots run deep,
A vision, one I vowed to keep.
This wasn't romantic, at least not that kind—
It was a journey that was all mine."

Her words had stung, though not meant to wound,
A reminder of how others presume.
For years, I've worked, with strength as my guide,
Building a life where I've stood satisfied.

But now, as I reflect on what I've achieved,
The homes, the dreams, the goals conceived,
I realize the proving is finally done,
And perhaps, now, I'm ready for someone.

Not to complete me, not to define,
But to share in the life that's wholly mine.
Still, it's strange how the world can't see,
That my worth is rooted in simply being me.

Let them misperceive, let them assume,
My journey is mine, with space to bloom.
And through it all, I'll stay hopeful, strong,
Knowing I've been on the right path all along.

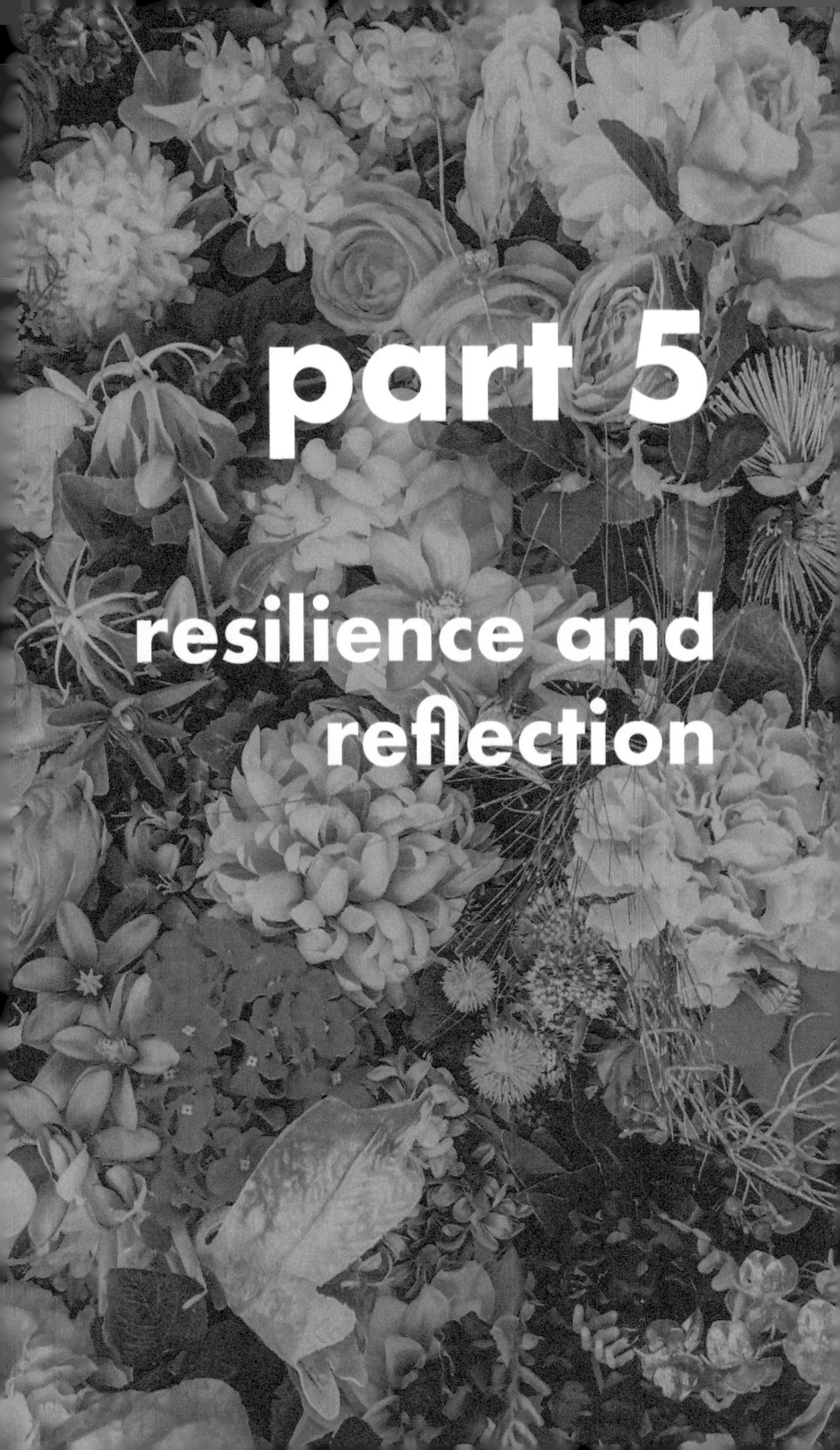

part 5
resilience and reflection

ladder 25

On West Seventy-Seventh, near Amsterdam's flow,
Ladder 25 stood, its courage aglow.
Next to my home, the men's laughter would rise,
Men of strength with kind, watchful eyes.

I walked by each morning, pregnant and free,
Exploring the city, my sanctuary.
The crew would wave, their voices warm,
"California girl, we'll brave any storm.

"When January comes, in the snow or ice,
We'll get you there, no need to think twice.
The fire truck's ready, our promise is true,
We've got your back, just call—we'll come through."

But that promise, so simple, so light in tone,
Became a wish carved in stone.
For September arrived, skies turning smoky gray,
And Ladder 25 answered that day.

The morning crew left, their duty clear,
And the city dissolved into chaos and fear.
She watched from her window, her heart in her throat,
As the city's grief wrapped her like a heavy coat.

The afternoon crew, with resolve so raw,
Returned to the rubble of what they saw.
Searching for brothers they'd known so long,
Hoping to find them, praying they'd been wrong.

Covered in soot, shoulders bent low,
How could men of such strength look so shadowed, so low?
Their brothers were gone, their spirits torn,
The firehouse, a place of both courage and mourn.

Each January, her child was born anew,
But September came, with its somber hue.
Wherever she wandered, whatever the year,
She'd find a firehouse to honor those dear.

With food and flowers, a heartfelt note,
She shared her gratitude, the words she wrote.
"Ladder 25, always by my side,
Though fate had a different plan to guide.

"You stood when the world was falling apart,
Your courage still beats within my heart.
I honor your spirit, fierce and true,
Year after year, I remember you."

Sometimes a hug, sometimes shared pain,
Sometimes silence, just soot in the rain.
But always, their strength, their sacrifice stays,
Echoing loud through her life's winding ways.

For Ladder 25, their courage profound,
Lives on in her steps, in the lives they surround.
In every firehouse she finds, there's a spark,
A reminder of light born from the dark.

awake in the dark

Still learning the tide, the year
After my grandma died.
Loss was fresh, a wound still raw,
And then your passing broke what I saw.

We were opposites in so many ways,
You, cautious, steady with measured days.
I, the one who took the leap, whose fire ran deep.

But you died recklessly, not as you lived.
A crash, a moment, no time to forgive.
And that weight on my heart refused to give.
Why wasn't it me? The thought would persist,
The adventurer spared, while your life was missed.

I was far away when it all came to be,
On a Greek island, restless, at sea.
Something stirred, though I couldn't yet name,
An unease that lingered, that never came tame.

I booked the next flight, rushed back home,
And found that the world had become unknown.
The friend who dropped me at the gate,
Gone in a flash, a cruel twist of fate.

What followed was haze, the details unclear,
Grief's heavy hand, its veils so near.
A eulogy spoken through trembling breath,
To honor your life in the wake of your death.

A week later, the truth came alive,
Reading the report with your mom by my side.
The hours I wrestled on that foreign shore,
Were the moments you left, forevermore.

Two lives entwined, though we couldn't see,
The unspoken bond, your presence in me.
For years I carried the weight of the why,
But now I hold love, though I still cry.

Opposites we were, yet the same at heart,
Two halves of a whole, though worlds apart.
And in the dark, I find you still there,
Guiding my steps, quiet and aware.

At twenty-one, I began to learn,
Moments are fragile and loss will burn.
But through the flames, your light remains,
A steady glow that life reclaims.

a view from the hills

She stands in the window, the city aglow,
Hollywood's lights, a shimmering show.
An iconic building, history steeped,
But tonight, her thoughts are heavy and deep.

The fires of '25 have taken their toll,
Smoke in the distance, a scar on her soul.
Even her home by the beach lies bare,
A memory now, ash in the air.

The city she loves feels foreign, changed,
Its parks now closed, its rhythm rearranged.
Arson's shadow, a lingering fear,
The future uncertain, the path unclear.

It stirs a memory, New York's dark day,
When towers fell, and lives gave way.
She'd found new love for a city that grieved,
Its strength in tragedy, hope retrieved.

But here in LA, a loneliness grows,
Among the hills and the evening's glows.
The city has shifted, its heart feels strange,
And she wonders aloud if it's time for change.

The ocean calls, its steady embrace,
A quieter life, a gentler pace.
Yet leaving feels like a bittersweet song,
For this city has held her for so long.

She weighs the options, her heart torn wide,
Between the hills and the tide.
To stay in the glow or follow the breeze,
To seek her peace among the trees.

For now, she lingers, the city her muse,
Haunted by loss, but searching for clues.
Making decisions, rebuilding her place,
With wonder to meet whatever she'll face.

the echo in her mind

The quiet hum of a post-pandemic day,
Alone with her thoughts, they drift and replay.
No office chatter, no passing smile,
Just a screen and a silence stretching the miles.

In this stillness, the echoes grow loud,
Voices of doubt, a relentless crowd.
"You're not enough," they whisper and sting,
Pulling at threads, unraveling her wings.

The ghosts of the past, their words still near,
Critiques once spoken, now amplified fear.
Old judgments linger, etched in her mind,
Stealing the confidence she fights to find.

Impostor syndrome creeps like a thief,
Turning triumphs to questions, joy into grief.
Every success feels like a mistake,
A house of cards she fears will break.

Isolation deepens the endless loop,
No voices to counter the inner troop.
No nods of approval, no "You're on track,"
Just time and her thoughts, a weight on her back.

But deep in her heart, a whisper remains,
A stubborn ember that pushes through pain.
"You've done this before; you can do it again,"
A quiet refrain, her mind's truest friend.

She writes down her wins, small though they seem,
Brick by brick, rebuilding her dream.
She reaches for hope, a call, a kind word,
Reminders of worth in voices heard.

Each day she battles, the shadows recede,
Replacing the doubt with the truths she needs.
Her path isn't easy, the struggle persists,
But her strength is a current that quietly insists.

For self-doubt may linger, but it cannot stay,
When courage and grace light the way.
And though the echoes may try to return,
She knows not to listen, to grow, to discern.

In a world gone quiet, she's learning to find,
Her voice, her power, her peace of mind.
Pushing forward, she builds her own proof,
A life that speaks louder than echoes of youth.

the last ride

She lands at JFK, her mind a haze,
Work calls buzzing, endless days.
A taxi summoned, her world on hold,
The city's pulse still loud, still bold.

On the phone, her voice stays firm,
While the driver steals glances, quiet, stern.
In the mirror, his eyes seem to say,
There's something familiar about this day.

When the call ends, he asks with care,
"Were you here in 2001's despair?"
She freezes, the past rushes back,
Memories carved in the skyline's black.

"You were the one," he says with care,
"That day when chaos filled the air.
I drove you then, you begged me to flee,
But you stayed calm—for my family and me."

She remembers now, the streets in despair,
Searching for friends who weren't there.
His cab was her refuge, his fear was her own,
Yet she told him to leave, to go back home.

"You promised me you'd get out alive,
Back to your wife, just survive."
"And I did." He nods, his voice now low,
"My wife thanks you more than you'll know."

Each year, they admit, they've thought of this day,
Of the woman who calmed him, who showed him the way.
"I'm grateful you're here, and safe, and well,
The stories we carry, the ones we tell."

As they part, the city looms near,
A moment shared, profound and clear.
Two lives entangled by that fateful ride,
Both survivors, still grateful, still tied.

through the stuckness

When you are stuck, just be—stuck still,
Embrace the weight; let it have its will.
Step outside; let the world breathe wide.
The caterpillar waits; the butterfly will glide.

It will be worth it, the waiting, the ache,
For beauty is born from what seems to break.
Through patience and stillness, a path will appear,
A moment of clarity, a release from fear.

Feel it within; let your body guide;
The suffering whispers where peace may hide.
Lean into the pain; Explore what it shows.
In the depths of sorrow, transformation grows.

Sense the emotion; give it a name.
Walk through the fire, through sadness or shame.
Madness will falter, the fear will subside,
And forward you'll move, with wisdom as guide.

the voices in my ear

I sit at home; the hours drift by,
A quiet world beneath the sky.
No office buzz, no coffee shop din,
Just me and the silence I'm living in.

Then come the voices, bright and clear,
A podcast stream to fill the ear.
Entertainment, knowledge, laughter, and cheer,
Strangers talking, yet they feel so near.

A host's enthusiasm lights my day,
Their stories keep the loneliness at bay.
Education whispers through the wire,
Igniting thought, sparking desire.

But sometimes, lines blur, truth bends thin,
I mistake their voices for places I've been.
In a chat with a friend, I'll pause and say,
"Remember when—wait, was that yesterday?"

No, it was them, those digital friends,
Whose banter and wisdom my mind defends.
Not faces I know, not hands I've held,
But companions in whose stories I've deeply dwelled.

And yet, the irony lingers in this place,
A soothing balm with a lonely trace.
For while they fill my solitary space,
They pull me inward, away from the face.

The warmth of strangers, the comfort they send,
Becomes both a healer and a trend.
Do I seek their voices, or seek a friend?
Do they connect me, or help me pretend?

grief's drive

When I was twenty, the world grew dim,
My grandmother gone, life seemed grim.
A year passed by, another blow,
A friend lost tragically, grief's shadowed glow.

I cried myself to sleep each night,
Yet rose each morning, seeking light.
The internet's dawn, my career took flight,
Selling dreams to Estée's might.

Highly functional, deeply torn,
Grief a cloak I silently wore.
Two years of tears, of aching stages,
Grief's journey filled endless pages.

Then decades spun, the losses grew,
My father passed, and pain renewed.
I held a friend through cancer's tide,
While children mourned their friend who died.

Through it all, I built and thrived,
Luxury dreams where I survived.
Head down, heart heavy, I forged ahead,
Success and sorrow tightly wed.

Now thirty years later, I pause, reflect,
See the threads of grief connect.
Each loss became a fire, a spark
That drove me forward in the dark.

seeking the lighter path

I look back on the life I've lived,
A tapestry woven, tight and vivid.
Threads of love, of work, of care,
Of joy that shone through, though sometimes rare.

There was a seriousness that shaped my days,
Decisions and duty to life's winding maze.
I've laughed, I've loved, I've danced, it's true,
But now I yearn for something new.

This second phase, an open door,
To seek what life still has in store.
Yet with it comes the weight I know,
Of losses to bear, of seeds to grow.

But even in grief, in struggle's embrace,
I want to find ease, to carve out space.
For joy in the simplest, laughter's release,
Moments that soften and bring me peace.

I'll put my energy into the air,
Sending out light, love, and care.
Creating a world within my reach,
Where joy and connection are what I preach.

To laugh more often, to let life flow,
To revel in beauty wherever I go.
To find the humor, the spark, the play,
In the everyday moments that shape my day.

Yes, the road ahead may test my heart,
But joy is a skill, an intentional art.
And I choose to practice, to seek, to try,
To live with light until I die.

i want

When my time comes, let it be
In a space of love, in harmony.
Surrounded by stillness, my dearest near,
My dog at my feet, no trace of fear.

As I take my final breath,
Let joy eclipse the weight of death.
Let hands come together, a gentle sound,
Clapping for the life I found.

For I lived authentically, fully, free,
A life of depth and meaning to me.
With resilience, I pursued my dreams,
A shining thread in life's grand seams.

Let my children feel pride, their hearts alight,
For I was their example, their guiding light.

A soul who loved, who dared, who gave,
Who lived well from cradle to grave.

And as I let this life slip by,
Peaceful, with no need to try,
Know I lived with beauty and let it show—
Then gracefully, I let it all go.

a meeting that changed the map

In New York, I climbed, my dreams alive,
A young woman rising, sharp and alive.
Running a division, stars in my sight,
Ambition burning in Manhattan's light.

I hit the marks; I played the game,
Corporate goals, a rising name.
But even in towers polished and grand,
Shadows can slip through a steady hand.

An acquisition loomed, tensions ran high,
A meeting was called—the full team, the why.
I arrived to find just him and a grin,
Flowers on the table, a trap pulled in.

My heart kicked hard, but I stayed composed,
Said, "Let's forget this,"—a deal I proposed.
"Tomorrow at work, we'll act as we should,
No harm done if this is understood."

But silence has teeth, and power strikes back,
Retaliation cloaked in whispers and cracks.
Later that week, crossing Madison fast,
He hissed, "If you'd slept with me, you'd have a better path."

The doors began closing, the invites grew thin,
Executive rooms I once sat within.
Meetings moved without my seat,
Success unraveled beneath my feet.

Young and afraid, I bore the weight,
Pregnant, weary, I chose my escape.
Leaving behind a map I had drawn,
Because no one would stand when the lines were wrong.

If it happened today, I'd rise and roar,
Face him square, demand much more.
Time has armed me with courage and flame—
No longer a girl who carried their shame.

And though it's my story, it's millions' more,
Ghosts in boardrooms behind closed doors.
Now voices rise, fierce and wide,
No longer afraid, no longer denied.

full circle

When I was young, behind a door,
I dreamed of life, of something more.
A world where love was always near,
where I could live beyond my fear.

I'd sketch and draw, I'd close my eyes,
and picture endless, open skies.
Each whisper held a seed of hope,
a quiet strength that helped me cope.

Through twists and turns, through pain and fight,
I chased the dreams born in the night.
And though the path was far from straight,
it led me here—my chosen fate.

The girl who once felt locked away
now stands within the light of day.
Her world is vast, her heart is free,
she's everything she dreamed she'd be.

Full circle now, the story told,
a life once fragile, now so bold.
From silent rooms to dreams made real,
a journey shaped by all I feel.

what i choose now

I have labored for this—
not just in the visible grind
of deadlines met and midnight ambitions,
but in the quiet labor no one sees:
the untangling of childhood knots,
the slow alchemy of silence into solace,
the architecture of peace,
built patiently from the inside out.

I have carved a life
that is wholly mine—
where I rise unburdened,
where my laughter rings true,
no longer borrowed from a past
I had to stitch back together.
I am not waiting for rescue,
nor piecing myself from shards.
I am whole.

Not because the path was kind,
but because I refused to abandon it.

And when I meet you—
you, with history still heavy in your hands,
unfinished chapters folded into your breath—
I see your heart.
I feel its pull.
But I also see the distance
from where I stand.

This is not judgment.
It is knowing—
that I have come too far
to welcome chaos where I have cultivated calm,
to exchange clarity for a storm
that is not mine to survive.

So when I say
that I choose the life I've built,
that I choose myself—
even as I hold you
in the light I once searched for—
it is not rejection.
It is reverence.
For what I have become.
For what I will not undo.

the turning

For the last twenty years,
we were told:
"Go inward."
"Find your worth."
"Love yourself first."
And we listened.
We meditated.
Journaled.
Booked retreats on mountaintops
and stared our shadows in the face.
We learned to sit with our pain,
name our needs,
unpack our childhoods,
walk ourselves home.
It was holy.
It was healing.
It was overdue.
But then—
the world stopped.

Doors closed.
Eyes turned further inward.
The self became
not just a place of reflection,
but a place of residence.
And we forgot how to come back out.
Now we swipe left on nuance,
ghost without grief,
confuse boundaries with walls,
and mistake disconnection
for growth.
We call it healing
when sometimes,
it's hiding.
We say we're protecting our peace,
but sometimes
we're just afraid to be known.
To be messy in front of someone.
To be seen in the becoming,
not just the polished aftermath.
There is a loneliness
no amount of self-love can cure—
the ache of not being mirrored,
not being witnessed,
not being held in real time
by real arms.
This isn't a dismissal
of the work we've done—
it's a call
to balance.
The next chapter asks more of us.
Not less introspection,
but more integration.
Not less healing,

but more humaning.
More table for two.
More "How are you, really?"
More sitting across from someone
and letting the silence be enough.
The future isn't solo.
It never was.
And maybe the bravest journey now
isn't farther in—
but finally,
back out.

the thread of maybe

We plan like architects of certainty,
drafting futures on fragile glass.
But life is weather—wild, unscripted,
shattering even the best-laid path.

Anxiety camps in the unknown,
pitching fear where clarity fades.
But when we loosen our grip on control,
the storm quiets. We find space.

The thread of maybe is not weak—
it flexes, bends, and refuses to snap.
It teaches us to dance without doubt,
to meet the dark with an open map.

There's power in the not-yet-formed,
in mornings that don't promise sun.
For when we stop needing guarantees,

we start becoming—
one breath, one risk,
one radiant undone.

Opposite page: Tamara outside the painted pool, designed in collaboration with Alex Proba, at the first Hill House property in Palm Springs, California.

about the author

Photo © Madeline Tolle, Los Angeles, California

Tamara Hill is the owner of Hill House Group, an interior design and development business that transforms properties into curated destinations rooted in beauty, culture, and experience. Tamara worked for over twenty years in corporate America, leading digital experience design firms at top advertising agencies and delivering innovative digital products for major technology, consumer, hospitality, and entertainment brands. After leaving corporate life, she became an entrepreneur, developing luxury properties in Palm Springs and Italy. These projects garnered press attention and showcased her talent for turning vision into reality and uniting community in beautiful and purposefully designed spaces.

www.ingramcontent.com/pod-product-compliance
Lightning Source LLC
Chambersburg PA
CBHW020245010526
44107CB00002B/98